# The Jade Bower
## New and Selected Poems

Copyright © 2008 Carol Leavitt Altieri
All rights reserved.

ISBN: 1-4196-5594-9
ISBN-13: 9781419655944

Visit www.booksurge.com to order additional copies.

# The Jade Bower
## New and Selected Poems

Carol Leavitt Altieri

# Dedication

For my sons, Frank and Michael, and in loving memory of my daughter
Alicia Ann Altieri
March 4 1962–August 8, 2008

"She was the best friend a person could ever have."
Haris Lender


Those who contemplate the beauty of the Earth find reserves of strength
that will endure as long as life lasts.

~Rachel Carson

# Contents

Dedication

**One**

Flag Hill / 1
Caring for the Land / 2
Delivering Milk and Eggs / 4
Pilgrimage / 6
My Coming to Visit You Dad, Continues / 7
Sister Island / 9
Portrait of a Sister / 11
Tonight / 12
East Andover Country, Wintertime / 14
Wedding, Spring, 1950 / 16
Mother / 17
*Trailing Arbutus*–Mayflowers / 19
Arriving at Another Place / 20
Mrs. Blanc, the Arc of a Day / 22
Spare the Elders / 25
Latest Grandson / 27
Alyssa, Granddaughter / 29
Climbing Mount Monadnock / 31
The Day After the Six Year War / 33
The Marginal Way / 34
Quick-witted Entertainer / 36
Microcosmos / 37
Bird, Blossom, Branch and Tree / 39
Orangutan-colored Day / 40
Millennium Grove, R.I.P. / 42
Human Nature and Animal Sympathy / 44

Blue-footed Boobies / 46

Methuselah's Grove / 47

Unearthly Indian Pipes / 49

Metamorphosis / 50

**Two**

Tulip Tree / 51

Vanishing Marshlands / 52

Waved Albatrosses / 54

White-bearded Manikin Fraternity / 56

Behold Great Trees / 58

Elegy for Mostar's Old Bridge / 60

Casting Out Roots / 62

Newly Discovered / 64

Australia's Rainforest Birds / 65

Costa Rica Rainforest Alchemy / 67

Hiking the Silversword Loop / 69

Red Maple Wetlands / 71

A Dream of Saving the Hammonasset River / 73

A Bit Down on Our Luck / 74

American Woodcock / 75

*Sanguinaria Canadensis*/Bloodroot / 77

A Day's Climb on the Coast of Cornwall / 78

At Ocean's Edge of Peggy's Cove / 79

Hummers in the Fast Lane / 81

Prevailing / 83

Pacific Coast Rain Forest / 84

Hammonasset Salt Marsh at Winter Solstice / 86

Under Strangler Tree Boughs / 88

Viewing Giant Tortoises on Galapagos / 90

An Acorn Whistle / 92

Florida's Blue / 93

Swept Away by Monarchs / 95

Gifts of the Season / 96

Wangari Muta Maathai / 98

**Three**

Arrivata, Hawksbills / 99

Darwin's Enchanted Kingdom / 100

Stand Alone Cedar at Hammonasset / 101

Morning Sojourn with Frogs / 103

Teardowns South of Route One / 105

Crows and Sycamores / 107

Sinking Boot Steps / 108

Lake District's Dry Stone Walls / 109

Riding the Chariot to the Divine:
Legendary Lord God Bird / 111

Libretto for Spirit Bear Wilderness / 114

Goldfinch Days / 116

Orcas' Opera: Prince William Sound / 118

Golden Frogs / 120

Jesus Christ Lizards of Esquinas / 122

Anatomy of Alaska Landscape / 123

Iceland Summer / 124

I've Been Traveling on that Interstate Highway / 126

Commander and the Spotted Owls / 128

Shoreline Showdown / 130

View From Our Backyard / 132

How Far Does the Poison Sink? / 134

Mountain Top Removal / 135

In Brazil's Rainforest Tribal Chief Marimo Fights Loggers / 137

Catch the Day's Celestial Farewell / 139

Some Resonating Notes / 141

Acknowledgments / 143

Special Thanks / 144

Bio / 147

# Flag Hill

dirt road up five mile hill
    goldenrod next to stalks of hay
    mingled with wild periwinkles
    a palomino galloped in pasture
    three sisters, dad and I chased Holsteins
    and Guernseys to barn for milking.

in barn calves sucked nipples
    milking machine squeezed out
    frothy white liquid like mother-of-pearl,
    cows switched tails in dad's face.

our farm offered us: milk, butter,
    cream, apples, pears, cherries, peaches
    nests of bluebirds, phoebes,
    bobolinks, meadow larks
    and a pond with gleaming frogs.

∼

my sister meets me in Flag Hill woodlands,
    where she and I kneel
    down, touch stones
    clear weeds from father's, mother's
    and sister's graves among lichens,
    cinnamon ferns and painted turtle,
    breathing our own metamorphoses.

eyes rimmed with shadow,
    light of distant days
    pouring through white pines.

# Caring for the Land

Savoring fresh earth and hay scent,
I hear Father's wheelbarrow roll over ground.
Overalls frayed, speckled with weed seeds,
he pulls greens, harvests carrots and beets
with notes of song,

all the verses of *Home on the Range*.
I shell peas on porch
watch his legs fold and back bend when he digs
deeply with trowel in rhythm
through layers of soil, grubs, and worms.

In his hands, he feels vegetables solid
textures. They'll nestle with apples we picked
for root cellar in foreseeing winter.

Heaven knows how much he is not aware
of the divine nature of his being.
Back and forth, trudging in and out of barn,
sacrificing his comfort for our welfare.

He hears ravens overhead beat their wings,
lament of mourning doves
reminding of chores and rituals undone,
the intricacies of connections.

To root out carrots and beets, he kneels, thinking
about his father who taught him to strive,
a voice out of deep silence, multiplied.

CAROL LEAVITT ALTIERI

# Delivering Milk and Eggs

Guernsey and Holstein cows cropped
shafts of hay as snow swirled
over our shoulders and Dad
hitched Sandy to sleigh.
My sister Bevy, eleven and I fourteen,
wound down dirt road coated
with fresh snow.

Dad stashed crates of eggs, dozens
under seats and quarts of milk aft.
Our palomino horse covered
with blanket pulled the sleigh.

Bevy and I walked to customers' back
doors, handed the milk and eggs,
collected empty bottles.
Some customers paid;
others put it on the books.

A Ford truck drove by, blew horn
spooked Sandy; forced sleigh
off shoulder. Our beloved horse
slipped on ice patch, legs flew
out sideways.
Sleigh tipped over, shattered!

At wood's edge, milk formed
impressionist clouds; dozens
of scrambled eggs
splattered on snow like patches
of wild mustard.

The truck drove on; no scavenger
angels appeared. We scurried
around retrieving little unbroken.
Over yolk-tinged snow, my father's
aged face haunted my youthful one.

We trudged Sandy
up mountainous terrain;
blizzard accompanied us home.
Strong winds hurled fragments of ice;
cut our spirits like a scythe.

# Pilgrimage

Sun lights the pathway funneling
into wild flowers and foliage.

Wood warblers glean and gyre
from blossoms along streams

and chorus frogs begin vesper
songs along the ridge and up the gorge

of canyons and hollows. The whir
of a barred owl's wings make an aerial

dive as it pursues a weakened mouse.
Sun dew, star flowers, vines entangle.

Silver-green lichen makes a lacey palette
on rocks and boulders.

Ripples splash in brook's swirls
and plunge into waterfalls.

Live oaks provide the pagoda tiers
casting their shadows over ferns

and ground pines. Across the marshland,
little blue heron, one leg resting in shallow

slough searches out the hidden fish
and mayflies in the current.

We honor every creature
in an act of artifice to prevail.

# My Coming to Visit You, Dad, Continues

even though you're in another
land today, between heaven and apple-
pear, peach orchard,
I see veins of your weathered
face and feel light
from your presence,
when I clutch
your hand
with middle finger
missing.

I help you reach
under chickens' breasts for eggs
after milking teats
of Holsteins and polishing
vermillion, lime, peach-colored
fruit for deliveries in town.

Do you hear maple sap
plinking pails
from spigots you set out
in March with saddle horse and sleigh
when we gathered
sap to turn liquid amber?

You were planting more
fruit trees and playing
your harmonica
while whip-poor-wills' voices
rose from woodlands.

THE JADE BOWER

I will return to visit you
in your serene pasture before
nightfall, where
the wealth you passed
on to me was reverence
for sacredness
of linked landscape.

# Sister Island Sestina

We wove necklaces of black-eyed Susans when we played in fields;
many times, I pulled little sister in a red wagon up our mountain.
When I was ten, she was five clouded by mother's shadow.
A mile from the nearest neighbor our farm like an island,
where winter and summer we delivered milk and eggs to cities,
fed chickens, milked cows, no time for sorrow.

Now sixty years later, I recognize her young sorrow.
She cut her arms with a razor while I scythed hay fields
with Dad. One time a doctor came to take her away to the city;
the sanitarium was waiting under whispering mountains.
For her, there was no escape; it was surrounded like an island.
Our family, haunted by my sister's susurrant shadows.

And now, I remember more than a shadow;
I visited the hospital for love, abated my sorrow
After watching mockingbirds on Highland Island.
At times, I would pick wild strawberries to give her from fields
and reminisce about our hikes up Stratford Mountain,
but I dreaded going to the sanitarium in that dark city.

I shivered with graveyard cold in the city;
revisiting her was like a sentence under shadow,
and I wished she could escape so we could hike our mountain.
When authorities refused, we were suffused with sorrow,
wondering would she ever again see wild flowers in fields
or would she struggle, drowning in the surge of the island?

Doctors tried to understand, but her divided mind kept her on islands
of hallucination, and I left for college, estranged in another city.
She could not remember picking berries in our field,
when she was locked in the hospital under grave shadows.
She could not separate from sorrow
and remember only the happy times on our mountain.

When our parents died, she became isolated, a mountain
lacking hope, left alone, struck by demons on islands
of despair. My new life and children would distract my sorrow.
Time galloped forward, drug messiahs transplanted her from city
to a home where she washes dishes, still under genetic shadow
of delusions wandering in a wilderness of darker fields.

Trapped inside her spirit's field of vision, hallucinations of devils
appeared in the city. Mountain climbing with a falling person, I'm reaching
for her hands but she vanishes, an island among shadows.

# Portrait of a Sister

She was the youngest of four and acted strange.
I wanted to be under my own shadow and didn't play with her.

Most often, she'd be an outsider in the other room.
We played musical chairs, no chair left for her.

When she grew to be sixteen, my parents diminished
by something indefinable stumbled on

for help in the dark. A heavy rain spiked and wind
seethed again on our New Hampshire farm.

In an old photograph of her from our time, closer
to the horse and buggy days, a Diane Arbus, off-kilter look.

Most often, seizures shook and her wounds opened
to absorb the grievous cold of separation.

Spinning toward the abyss, our parents moved her away
from home and signed her for a lobotomy.

Subverted with hallucinations, facing a crucible time,
She rampaged through the sanitarium trying to escape.

Overthrowing her desires, officials handcuffed her.

I learned very soon that I could look at the *gorgons'*
*gaze* and not turn to stone.

No one, but me, left to call and visit her now.

# Tonight

my father sounds restless walking the acres
of Flag Hill Farm. Has he crossed the cosmos
gone to other planets and returned?
He ought to be out in the garden harvesting.
Instead he's dawdling in heaven savoring
raven pranksters of the realm turn skyward.

How he runs from ghosts in dark air.

Who does he wish to see,
his wives, son, two daughters
who have journeyed away?
Does he want to pick the fruit
from the peach, apple, pear trees he planted?

His love for me feels like apple picking, feels
like sap running; ravens passing objects to one
another with wing tips touching, playing
on mountain ridge.

How he hid from ghosts who tried to plague him.

Spring water in the well is quenching
after haying.
Does he watch royal blue, amber-breasted
barn swallows build their nests on beams in barn
he once showed me?
I can still smell the sweet hay scent of our
barn and farmhouse.

Back to that time and place,
I visit the old creek deep in woods
passing time with my feet dangling in Frog Brook
trying to view the hornpout and trout.

I hope he unburdens and wrestles time back.

Someone tell the new businesses not to cut down
his orchards.

God, how his ghosts meander in dark air.

# East Andover Country, Wintertime

Fresh snow cleaves to high hills.
Squalls of winter blotch Kearsarge Mountain.

Valleys of pasturelands glint like angelica plants
where once Indian paintbrushes and goldenrods

spiked wild grass. Brown oak and maple leaves
twist and turn around as shades of dried beech

leaves cling to limbs. Now hay stubble haggards
dry for winter.

My sister and I gather eggs and drop some in snow
like mustard flowers under boots.

In the barn, calves and pigs shelter by mothers
and shimmy to suckle.

The milk cans we filled perched on banks waiting for dairy
dealer threaten to topple over when snows shift.

In the parlor my father plays harmonica music
with my sister on the piano sending melodies

like rivulets of winnowing winds. Next year I hope
the larks and bobolinks return to mould their grass

nests in meadows and plough lands. When I leave
for another home, will I ever see a setting

like this again, the honeycomb of colors, pattern
and rhythm in a John Constable landscape?

CAROL LEAVITT ALTIERI

# Wedding, Spring, 1950

In front of tan-colored, stucco farmhouse,
view beyond apple orchard. Our mother
wearing Greta's dress, hand-on-hip resolute
in *listen-to-your-mother* pose.

Older sister, only seventeen, faithful
to mother's wishes wearing navy suit,
with translucent veil falling from blue
pillbox hat.

Justice-of- the-peace
offers testimony and ring rites
and friends read New and Old Testament
Bible verses.

One witness plays wedding music on 78's.
Our crank up phonograph keeps skipping.

I wear a shirtwaist flower dress. Clenching
hands, my younger sister and I stand aloof.
We would rather be somewhere else. Who
on earth will help them, I wonder?

A sacrificed bride with bouquet of rose-colored
peonies, dressed for a journey. My father
in shiny, dark suit and unshined shoes
grimaces, eyes red. Tendons standing out,
he turns his face.

# Mother

She wore old flower-printed house
dresses with hand-knitted
sweaters when you went
to Bible reading classes.

Puffed above her pale blue eyes
light brown hair streaked grey
rolled into waves.

Perhaps she had too many children,
too many pains
and too many farm chores.
Did she ever long for anything
in the Sears Roebuck catalog?
Did she ever have enough
money to buy
some stylish clothes?

She prevented us all our lives
from spending too much
and now I want
to join her, signing the compact,
*Not Buying It: One Year
Without Shopping.*

In the nursing home,
when she could talk
she asked to come live with me.
I reddened
like her scarlet geraniums
when I couldn't comply.

She has been away for twenty-five
years and I still wish I could tell her
how many trees I've saved.
But she is blessed to be with her God
in Calvary Cemetery where butternut
trees she protected
will be safe by stone walls,
not far from Flag Hill farm.

## *Trailing Arbutus-* Mayflowers

My mother brings a bouquet to me,
most treasured, newly-sprouted mayflowers.
In April, sweet fragrance from forest edge,
like rarity of bloodroot or yellow ladyslippers.

Trailing leathery leaves and woody stems
peeking and pushing from spring
earth, hiding under heart-shaped leaves.
The earliest, tinged pink, spread their petals,
perfumed and spry, ushering in spring.

Mayflowers lead way for lilacs, columbines,
trilliums, Quaker-ladies, and Solomon's seals.
All join the woodland show,
bowing like courtiers before a queen
and I hear rills and ripples
of the Isinglass River.

Breathe deeply and inhale the fragrance
symbolizing deep unspoken love.
In shady places of clumps and patches,
flowers commingling with earth,
scent and apple blossom essence.

In heaven now, my mother clutches
a bouquet of mayflowers. Some wildflowers linger
in pockets of mind,
I cultivate their sanctuaries for retreat.

"Our attachment to the land was our attachment to each other."
<u>Refuge</u> by Terry Tempest Williams

## Arriving at Another Place

Some fifty years ago, I tramped home
   from school, holding my arms open for my little sister.

Today, leaning on a crutch,
   my younger sister manages to hobble out/
     out of the group home.
All winter she has been waiting for me
   to take her out to the Ice Cream Shop
     for glazed donuts and strawberry sundaes.
She wants to taste the moment as another
   sweet and chocolate candy bar.

We arrive at the old homestead
   where she once gathered Lilies of the Valley
     by our two-room grammar school.
Some vision in my mind
   of father, mother and other younger sister stirring
     in buried grounds calls me.

I found our childhood farmhouse on Flag Hill
   with barn roof caved in next to overgrown orchard.
Nearby, the family's cemetery harbors phantoms
   drifting in white pine grove and fading sunset
     by bloodroot and purple trillium.

What keeps her waiting in the car unwilling to get out?
    I ask her, "*Why do you always*
        *stay inside?*"
"*A prosecutor has marked me*
    *for extermination. Take the orders*
        *off me!*" she pleads.

"*Remember how I used to child sit with you?*"

    I kneel, planting meadow asters beside the graves.

## Mrs. Blank, the Arc of a Day

When I'm thinking of staying another hour
    under the covers, as surely as day breaks,
        she leaves the serenity of her home,

her wild flower garden and waves of roses.
    mourning doves sing splashes of joy
        and spires of evergreens lift arms to sunlight.

Driving her arthritic body,
    she appears beside the station
        wheeling her brief case

en route to work in Manhattan
    like a meteor moving slower
        but burning always brighter on a trail.

Week after week, we trade notes
    and community news
        traveling along our diverse routes.

I tell myself, *I hope her spirit will light on me.*
    Ninety-five years old and still steeped
        in desire, passion, and wisdom.

Memories of five children and ten grandchildren
    fed one of her specialties,
        butternut squash gnocchi.

True to the poet, Kunitz, ever-seeking
    transcendence, after mother, father, and husband
        fell from her life along the way.

She is still devoted to her
    layers helping the human spirit thrive:
        gourmet, gardener, patron, altruist, visionary.

Surely as I look for the evening star,
    unaware of my arrival, she returns to station,
        having cast staffs of schools and hospitals.

Constellations glimmer in the heavens above.

THE JADE BOWER

## Spare the Elders

A crown of leafy branches
cradles a pair of marbled
murrelets sending out a whistling
cadence to the heavens.

Then the slash-and-burn ones
come with their bulldozers,
chainsaw gangs and gold miners,
swabbing pepper spray on our eyeballs
bringing harvesters and skidders
to the largest stands,
sequoias and redwoods
alive for over a millennium.

All day until the setting sun,
sixty-foot band saws
with blades and skidders
pulling trees to loader;
the fellerbuncher
like a huge scissors strip
trees in two giant bites;
grabs the hard, the soft,
the saplings, the living and the dead.

The earth splits and shakes
under root fibers.
Broken spiders dangle
by chipmunk babies ripped out of nests.
And the Black-throated Blue Warblers
in their moss–hair nest

from newly hatched eggs
are crushed on their first quest.

Skidders and bunchers revving,
cracking, roaring down the runway:
earthmovers stripping soil,
suffocating gills of salmon,
clogging streambeds of frogs.
Chipping and pulping
leaving gray stubble of humps.

What's left
after Solomon's seal, wild ginger,
blood root are crushed,
Douglas firs, ponderosa
saplings; pine sprouts ripped
from the soil?

A butchered landscape
with piles of burned slash;
an automatic rifle resting
beside a battered tree stump,
in front of blackened horizon.

# Latest Grandson

Blessed with six
grandchildren,
all of them from another
time frame,
and that has changed me
to see my little part of the planet
in a transformed light as I adore
the seventh.

The voice of impermanence
hassels me and still I exult
in being here in my ageless years
as changes occur in mind and body.

I gain strength and gather joy
through love of infants recalled
as they nestle in contours
of my arms and breast as sculpture
of Indian story teller.

I pick him up and hold him gently
and envision him cuddled
in a hawthorn wreath.

First awakening of nature
bonds us and draws the pattern
for our lives. Joy ripples
as we watch the robins give birth and
young fledge away.

## THE JADE BOWER

I wonder if my grandson and I will linger
with Robert Frost at edge of woods
and trek up Mount Katahdin with Thoreau.
Surely the voices of hope and longing
inspire me like winding waves of wisteria
on pergolas and thresholds.

## Alyssa, Granddaughter

Mornings in Vermont, with three others sleeping
in one bed Alyssa enlivened our awakening

as grandfather spread out cereal, bagels with cream cheese
in our cottage room at Smuggler's Notch.

I looked closely at her head on the pillow and admired
her beauty mark next to bluebell eyes with

long brown hair, loosely brushed over intense gaze,
ears adorned with rosettes.

For a while, I dwelled on my memory of her as a little girl
carried in a bicycle trolley by her father on Martha's Vineyard.

Under an aura of woodland trees, meadow lands, rocky
cliffs, trails to sandy beaches, thundering shores

of the Atlantic and fishing trips to the Maine seacoast,
she waved the banner of life.

∼

But today, we are home in our yard smelling the fragrance
of the air like herbal balm from branches of evergreens.

She and her sisters under rays of the sunbeams
help plant our back yard sanctuary growing fuller

with swooping birds, butterflies, pulse of fishes
and frogs romping in the pond.

I feel the shifting ground of farm life I grew up on
and resolve to be around to see the three sisters

rise to make their nests of discords and melodies.
We entwine our lives together quenching desires

that would not let us drift from rich earth

-so close to sea from shore.

# Climbing Mount Monadnock

In September, with Bethany Wanderers,
after the season of Frost's purple-fringed
orchids, I trudge
the blue trail of Monadnock.

Hungry for the taste of the hard
and the real, lugging backpacks,
we rub elbows with hikers,
mountaineers, climbers,
adventurers and seekers.

Scrambling, catching our breath
we climb rock stairs:
backs straining, toes burning,
muscles stretching,
treading tables of granite
between rock outposts.

I stop to view terrain
of fissures under
birch, beech, and maple trees.

Mountain streams strive
past tattered curtains of hemlock,
sweet fern and sheep laurel.

Meadow voles, shrews, hairy moles,
lynx eyes shine from secluded dens.
Above, black-capped chickadees
pass on their legacy.

Among bracken, fern, sumac,
deer moss and partridgeberry, we strain
and stumble dodging the falling rocks.

## THE JADE BOWER

Sun striking, I struggle up terrain,
skid over stairway of ledges,
push myself over rock ribs,
cave in, crawl and fall under pitch
pine. Other hikers strive on.

Fellow climbers reach summit's spine
where natives drank sarsaparilla
and smoked peace pipes.

I drink vistas stretching eastward
and westward feeling infinitesimally
small in space as a cricket flickers
and chants in prickly pear.

And I think about all the wild
life having mating embraces
after we have returned home.

# The Day After the Six Year War

As far as I can see, no mountain tops,
clear rivers or streams. Lampposts and clocks

like Dali paintings folded and in pieces.
Cargo of cement and uprooted trees

burn and pile over one another.
I taste charcoal and oil burning on dust.

Dump sites and broad universe of sediment
layer the worn-out land along with torsos and heads.

Fecund smells as street cleaners sweep
up fingertips and flesh scraps.

Twisting lines of weeds poke heads up. Last night,
a silver moon flickered passing in and out of gray cover.

Lost, hungry, thirsty, my unit killed, I try hard to find
something edible, not allowing any memories

to enter my mind. In the mist, a child's kite trails
a long forked tail behind. I hear a bird and raise

my binoculars to scan naked tree limbs. *That's
a lifetime bird for me! No one alive to tell it to.*

No leaves from trees layer to heal earth's torn flesh.

# The Marginal Way, Ogunquit, Maine

Mid- morning fog lifts. My daughter and I
bound together from different spheres,
feel pull of moon on ocean's tide

on rocky outcrops heaving out of coast.
Near cliffs where glaciers gouged retreat,
we pause on pathway, sit on the bench

as my sister and I once did
sharing Coleridge's,
"The Rime of the Ancient Mariner."

Today dwellings slope to hidden beaches,
and children explore tidal pools of slate-blue
mussels and rosy crabs in flotillas

of seaweed. Wary of slick-covered
downward slanting-boulders,
a giant snail's trail, we view

the ocean's glow of cobalt blue
writhing away to the horizon. My daughter's hair
glistens with sunlight like my sister Beverly's

forty-five years ago. Essence of wild roses
and beach plums cover rocks.
Crashing surf in high swells

sounds against domes of granite and schist.
Hymns—emerge from shrubbery
as swallow-tailed piping plovers wearing

black stripes on shoulders and brow
come soaring in on ocean tides
whistling their lonely notes.

Plovers flutter in circles and cuddle on rocky cliffs,
feathered wings clutching mates and chicks;
seeking green sea urchins that puff up spines

like porcupines. They anchor themselves to rocks
in ocean water, clear as a quartz crystal
flowing in tidal pools, most potent amber.

# Quick-witted Entertainer

Our catbird
wearing black cap,
dark gray over light,
rusty brown under tail,
flicks about in bull briers,
loving the red mulberry.
Ventriloquist: mewing, croaking
clicking cricket arias
in a many-tongued, comedy.

Nesting in shrubbery
he perches nearby,
laughs with me while
listening to his cousin,
the mockingbird sings in
hawthorn tree. He pauses,
sputters and hisses
the mocker's song.

Having the limelight
composer and improviser:
cackles, chuckles, connives.

My rollicking companion
singing for his dinner,
struts impresario,
increasing the magic
of the avian world.

# Microcosmos

You will see no advertising here-
no exotic shimmering leaves,
no charismatic species,
but you will see pond snails
brown and gray-toned
with sand-colored grains
and clear water reflecting caddisflies
entwined with underwater nymphs.

You will find northern dusky salamanders,
quiet, nimble, delicate as snow drops
hiding beneath mossy stones,
rare, hidden and unadorned.

Turn over the stone and pick one up:
long-tailed, ridge on top,
floating on lily pads
brown and gray-toned with sand-colored grains.

A miracle of eternity revealed
as you gently hold *northern dusky's* fragile body,
trying to sense the breath
of its skin flowing across your cupped palm

She swivels and shimmies, rhythmic like an eel,
swerving tiny fingers and hind
limbs to free herself,
and squirms away.

# THE JADE BOWER

She knows how to slip below
the surface of an egg-laying adventure
and live an orderly, purposeful life.
She does not need to conjure up a spell
or send out a sound,
as she gyrates down in an honorary kingdom.

# Bird, Blossom, Branch and Tree

Wandering down a country path
seeing the small violets at my feet,
I wonder about the design of a butterfly;
think about the redstart in green
alpine meadow.

Winding through valley and refuge
touch the intricacy of a warbler's feather;
feel the willowy river breezes
and the sun canopy that warms me.

Ponder about the age of pyramids
built when the sequoia was a sapling;
cathedral spires reaching skies
shaping spiritual landscapes.

Muir's trees of life
housing spirits and saints;
now vanishing forests shorn
for pulp. It takes a hundred years
to grow the heartwood.

# The Orangutan Colored Day

There is that time
in the jungle of Sumatra
   when I witnessed
an anguished face
   bespeaking our kinship.

∼

A glimpse of *Spiritus Mundi*:

High forehead, jutting jaw;
deep-set, soulful eyes
   scintillate.

Auburn-burnished fur
   brushed over blue blood
glides above my raised eyes
   under somber shadows.

Loud chatter fills the air
   as he swings on branches
     calling for his mate and son.

For a cradle,
   he weaves branches and vines;
holds a *rafflesia* leaf over head
   performing aerial acrobatics.

At the fruit tree banquet,
   when the hornbill snatches figs,
he shrugs, grabs a pine tree,
   reaps heart of palm.

Still longing for family, he barks
    for mate and infant.
Spooked, he growls
    and gnashes his teeth.

∼

I yearn for *Spiritus Mundi*,
    but human raiders come,
conspire, capture....

## Millennium Grove, R.I.P.

Giant Sequoias, Temples of Time,
I offer you fragrant frankincense,
for thousands of years of growth
in forests of cedars, Douglas firs,
spruces and ponderosa pines.

Ferns genuflect under your canopies
like priests swinging
braziers of burning myrrh.
You were seedlings and saplings
when Neolithics lugged giant
stones for Stonehenge.

Groves of your ancestors sheltered
nomadic wanderers.
A crown of branches cradle
a pair of rare murrelets
sending out whistling cadences
to the visitors.

You hold spotted owls,
offer shelter to salamanders
and save spawning salmon.

Then your limbs are lopped off
and song sparrows are bloodied
silenced in their nests.
A revving of chainsaws storms
your temples as trees plunge
and smash forest-loving creatures.

Earth movers chain your arms,
pull trunks up by roots,
drive from the scriptorium
and you are scavenged
to a mill that grinds your temples
up for pulp.

# Human Nature and Animal Sympathy: an Illusion of Victory

Do you remember the night ramble
    seeing the lights of fireflies,

lines of meteors and hearing
    thunder-pumping bitterns?

For some eight years of struggle,
    we were high with hope

to save golden tidal marsh acres
    island trees and all abiding creatures

cocooned in their homes.
    What made us reach so far

and dance so wildly?
    Wind birds silhouetted against the moon?

Belief, passion and hope,
    belief, passion and hope....

longing to protect a once pristine land.

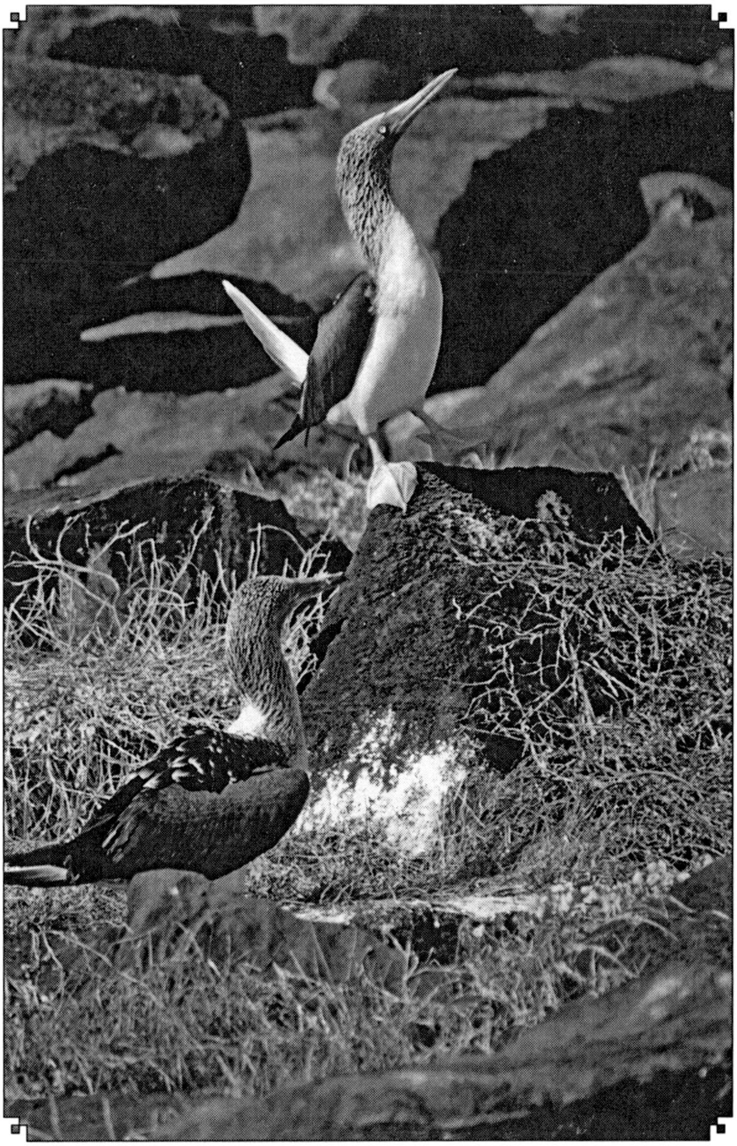

# Blue-footed Boobies

On Darwin's uplifted Galapagos,
on intertwined branches
male and female blue-footed boobies
salute each other, high stepping
and flaunting blue suede shoes
in a lindy hop; then a dude jitterbug.

The *King of Swing* in prom dress
pirouettes around her angling
his bill upward. She sways her neck
around as he sends up a shrill whistle.

She utters a cooing reply.
He shakes, rattles and rolls among land
iguanas on volcanic tuff.

Together, they make rounds of nesting
grounds, reconnoiter among tortoises
enchant audience and embrace on stage.

# Methuselah's Grove

Spires of evergreen arms,
contorted and crooked
for millennia
(even before Lebanese cedars
from Biblical times)
sent out scriptures.

Seeds swept by ancient winds
grew into golden boughs
striated with dark strands;
evaded brutal storms
and the harsh world.

With strolling acolytes,
I roamed the range for blessings,
touched bristlecone
contorted shapes
ascended dry landscapes
wound in and out of dolomite spires
and rocks worn smooth
from previous pilgrims.

A whole universe writ
in Cosmic Trees.

Fortress-like,
protecting the delicate eggs
of the Townsend's warbler
and varied thrush
whose snug nests
in deep-green pine needles

among prickle-tipped cones
sequester for another season.

Never were trees so sculpted
by sacraments of drought,
lightning, wind and fire.

Here festooned with green-blue
lichen, they shelter juniper,
incense cedar,
and wild flowers embraced by stones
reflecting mountain light.

# Unearthly Indian Pipes

Out trudging in deepest woods
one early evening,
a pair of wild flowers unfurling,
reveal Indian pipes,
standing straight
exalting in white translucency
in summer woodlands.

I'm anxious that they might have been
trampled over by fellow walkers.

No, they are there again,
just as I found them last year
pushing up and embracing
in the shadow of the beeches.

Ghostly, mysterious from another time
in deepest darkest niches
clusters of waxy stems
whorl in miniature petals.

Living on woodland floor,
not casting off
waste products of detritus;
sharing relations with a fungus
like an evolving human
cross pollinating to perfection.

# Metamorphosis

I begin as a painted wood turtle
whose shell in concentric
ridges protects my green limbs. I prowl
over fields and woodlands under my impregnable
shell relishing wild strawberries.

In the tulip tree, with twigs touching,
I become a sharp-witted northern oriole,
in robe of flame-orange
bold-black, and radiant gold. I browse
in cherry blossoms, crafting my talents
into nestlings' hanging basket.

Soon I become a dipper
that hides lichen-fern nest
under the waterfall to keep chicks
protected. I bound out, dive deep down
fetching water striders.

Now I am
a salamander
whose blue polka-dotted skin
reflects my eyes as I feed on algae skeletons
and plankton filaments.

In part of the world unpaved,
Arethusa, nymph of spring arrives; sun shines
and warms the moist ground. Then I metamorphose
into the magenta, rare flower of the East, a lady slipper.
Orchid photographers discover me and swear
to secrecy my place.

# Tulip Tree

Self-seeded,
one old-growth left in our domain
that survived geological changes,
hewed canoes of natives,
and hireling engines of bulldozers.

Between the frog pond and bluebird house
(where five chicks fledged)
our tulip tree thrusts its ribbed bark upward
columnar, higher than
Mohegan Sun Casino.

Swaying in backyard breeze,
leaves and blossoms flicker lightly,
a haven for romancing Baltimore orioles
and swallowtail butterflies.

Creamy sapwood;
winged seeds rustle
and intertwined branches offer
golden and ochre tulip blossoms,
a glowing candelabra.

# Vanishing Marsh Lands

Early morning rises like a sleeping bear.
I wade in, weave my way through sedge
hummocks of cattails, spartina and cord grass.

How loyal tides
surge and recoil from the sea
seducing me here with plants cloaked
in shades of beige-gold, emerald and lavender
shaped into whorls.

Two kinglets flash crowns
in wildlife banquet alive with calls.

Eastern kingbirds in breeding livery launch
air raids pursuing dragonflies.

And there among the reeds, rare seaside
sparrows sing another rendition.

And deeper down in layers, bluefish
and striped bass in different waters
chase in the tide for mummichugs.

I hunt green and pickerel frogs hearing them
trill and seduce females among washed up stones.

Then I spy my totem, a diamond-back terrapin.
I feel his pulse
as I ask forgiveness for wounds
of his species

as he lumbers away toward
Route 1.

I'm ashamed that I cannot save its destiny
along unnatural pathways
once a marshland.

# Waved Albatrosses, Galapagos

At edge of Espanola, my kayak
splashes ashore as penguins
rise to skim the waves.

Above, great frigate birds
like gymnasts try to snatch fish
from red-billed tropic birds.

When moon is full at high tide,
I scramble over magma,
scan the edge of the lagoon
where waved albatrosses perform
wild mating rituals.

Like hang gliders, singly and in colonies,
they land among palo santo trees.
Golden, buff-brown bodies
beaks with yellow tubes
and black button eyes,
for nocturnal fishing.

In mid-April, males return
from sweeping far ends of earth
from open seas.

In aerial ballets they cut air
arrange their nesting sites
for collective orgies with females
until a mate for life is enticed.

Beaks clack-clack-clack and cross,
like affectionate duelers.

The partners mew,
bob heads, twirl
raising tube noses
inspiring love
as Pavarotti's singing Rossini's
La danza.

# White-bearded Manakin Fraternity

Before twilight where hill
ascends valley 10,000
feet above sea level,
I climb in deep, green
rain forest of Asa Wright's
to see a communal party
of chickadee-sized
birds perform
on their courtship *lek*.

I spy on chunky birds,
as they prepare to hold court.
See one shuffle sideways,
whirring and snapping
picking up pebbles, feathers,
and twigs from his patch of land.
Other cocks-of-the-walk clear
ground, allowing not a speck
of debris to settle there.

Males cluster
in rakish, cocked crest,
ebony, well-packed suits
trimmed with arctic white.
They rub wings together
like bows across fiddles.
The inner piper plays as they strut,
hop scotch and sock hop
to and fro across court.

Orange-legged manakins
flash and swirl in blazes of ardor
and hoist skyward
to natives playing
steel drums.

# Behold Great Trees

From a minute seed
to a tall giant
overcoming indignities:
hurricanes, drying winds,
droughts, fungus, diseases,
ravages of pests and jobbers.

A great chestnut stood outside
where Ann Frank hid.
Here birds and organisms
sought shelter
and nested protection.

It has earned its place,
it has paid its dues
It was here before you
and with luck will be here
after you.

The world works better
when it doesn't lose its pieces.

CAROL LEAVITT ALTIERI

# Elegy for Mostar's Old Bridge

Harjudin of Dubrovnik
built a bridge across the Neretva
linking cities to hinterlands
when Suleiman the Magnificent
ruled Constantinople.

Masons quarried stones
dragged them down the riverbank
on sleds pulled by draft horses;
poured molten lead to cement blocks.
A shifting symbol of Ottoman control
bridged generations
of Serbs, Croats, and Bosnians.

Once I visited the bridge
and praised its soaring structure
of glinting white,
river-smoothed and moss-covered stones
over full-throated blue waters.
Because it suggested infinity,
I thought it would always endure.

Over 400 years, the bridge soared
and survived until neighbor
turned against neighbor
and drove opponents' community
across the Neretva.
Shelling continued,
and continued, and continued,
first pock marking; then convulsing
the old bridge.

*Golgotha of cleansing
as tanks and artillery chased
neighbors house by house
at point blank range and promise
of a Greater Serbia collapsed.
Tanks shook the earth
as artillery fired down;
dropped the bridge
like a Tyrannosaurus
into rushing blue-black waters.*

## Casting Out Roots

I

Along our sanctuary where Hammonasset runs,
a *Limited Liability Corporation* invades,
and bears false testimony for mansion city,
crowding out tidal river zone
that connects marshlands
and feeding migratory
routes and habitats.

Selectmen and associates bury
letters of protest and separate us from shoreline
by a corridor of SUV's, hummers,
and triple trailer trucks.

One selectman says, *birds
must accommodate to our life style.*

Condos and urban apartments five stories high
block views, so we can not hear or see seaside
and sharp-tailed sparrows, piping plovers, blue
herons, bitterns, golden sandpipers, or king rails.

II

At Hammonasset, stars of wild flowers animate
wooded glen with trilliums in roundelay.
Bulldozers devour mulleins, milkweeds, thistles,
clover, Indian paintbrush, asters, wild carrots,
lady slippers, mayflowers, marsh marigolds, roots
struggling underground to grow unseen.

No haven for oak tree, beach plum, fluttering marsh
wren, moss weaver, cord grass, and cattail.
Hermit crabs in secluded homes
with pairs of startled eyes stick out of mud.
Painted turtles are helpless, before backhoes.

I am the bloodroot bleeding where the oaks fall.

# Newly Discovered

Not seen for over a century, elusive to outside world,
two honeyeater birds in black, metallic plumage

with white glistening patches ascend to canopy.
Shining bodies flit around and hide in moss-

covered saplings. Six-wired birds of paradise
with wiry plumes and neon wisps of feathers

from head to tail follow whims of breezes.
They flutter sunstruck wings like Chinese fans;

whistle songs, make the forest swirl, scatter jewels,
and set me on fire. Rare creatures in rainforest

mountains of New Guinea as close to Garden
of Eden as you're going to find on Earth.

# Australia's Rainforest Birds

Out on the bird safari,
I breast surf in ferns
as rainbow lorikeets, reflecting
iridescent purple-green
angle downwind to oleander nectar.

Riding the kingdom's waves,
blue-winged kookaburras
in royal velvet cloaks
splash down in radiance.
Cousins, paradise kingfishers
flaunt tail streamers in canopy.

Congregations of rose gulahs,
slide on gusts of wind,
play a hymn to spirits,
rejoice acappella.

Filling cathedral of upper boughs,
eclectus parrots
hum on flutes
of eucalypti bringing messages
of morning news.

Like kites on tethers
yellow-tailed black cockatoos
suspend in cloudless sky.

Rainbow bee-eaters haunt
interior in sharp relief,
excelling in grace and flight.

THE JADE BOWER

Threading my way, I spin around
to admire the golden bowerbird.
He puffs his chest, raises himself,
displays bronze feathers,
swaying like a Greek dancer,
slapping wings in hypnotic rhythm,
and quickening virtuosi
of heart's rhythm.

# Costa Rica Rain Forest Alchemy

Early misty morning opens
in Talamanca Mountains
through double rainbow.

Buttress trees draped with mosses
and bromeliads grow heavy as lavender
orchids reach up to catch rain. Strands
of lianas weave the forest together.

Looking down in soft layer of litter,
a witch's brew of legs and arms.
Red-eyed tree frogs, beautiful wood nymphs
reddish- yellow with blue-jean legs
fight over breeding rights
luring females-
encircling forelimbs
embracing
in piggy- back position
clasping under armpits
sheltering under curled leaves.

Round the bend, sun angles on slopes
to flights of hyacinth macaws.
And higher up, in a courtship dance
emerald toucanets with yellow beaks
echo frog-like croaks.

Next to me, blue morphos flash fluorescent
wings, circle
and plummet down drunk with nectar.

Here, under the canopy, soaring
into dizzying spirals, I feel
the breath of wings and swing
of rain into sun.

# Hiking the Silversword Loop

On the cinder lava landscape
nourished by scrunchy soil
on Sliding Sands Trail
of Haleakala,
a spiky haired Silversword

stroked by Menehunes'
spiral wands
and nectared by orange
butterflies. Flowers fragile
as Perseid meteors
streaked white
across the sky.

They were taken to the Orient
for dried bouquets
uprooted by mountain goats
rolled like snow balls
over the trail.

Some looked like spun
glass ornaments after a fire.

Emerging slowly
from lava landscape
silk candles shimmered
in misty dusk.

# THE JADE BOWER

# Red Maple Wetlands

Beyond the throughway
behind our Audubon Shop
a fragment of rich woodlands;
a brook flows under fallen leaves,
where developers see condominiums.

Here I seek solace with painted turtles,
salamanders and other wetland creatures
alive among shadows.

I raise my binoculars
to look at luminous maples
and blue heron nest. First-year herons
hungry for fish and frogs glide down
landing along the stream.

Rufous-sided towhees
search and scratch warily
in undergrowth of cat's briar.

Above, eastern kingbirds sweep
sunlit crowns chasing iridescent
dragonflies.

The sun reminds me to leave but I stay
to watch for one last time
the burrowing of painted turtles
and non-Odysseus hatchings.

Just then, a stream of thrushes
like flutists fluting pass overhead.
Others will meet tonight
to change the wetlands' boundaries.

I stand here transported
from a scale of human terror
that all this life cannot comprehend.

# A Dream of Saving the Hammonasset River

*You cannot step in the same river twice; fresh waters are always flowing.*
                                    ~ Heraclitus, 500 BC

My talismans, piping plovers and roseate turns
    endure marathons, bear nestlings, spread wings
and become wind borne
    on tidal river's ebb and flow.
A multitude of voices cast a prolonged chorus...
I hear the melody of rich, resonant notes,
    hunker down
    in the blind and hear the season's voices of faith.

The preacher, a crested kingfisher splashes
    on river's crest and tide.
Framed by a cerulean sky, a braided
    tributary yields salt hay and eelgrass.
Marsh meadows offer oases
    for winged messengers, their bodies full,
wings spread wide. Stalks of spartina
    hide turtles and toads. A ringed bog haunter
quenches hunger and thirst from ripples.
    Pools and rivulets alternate downstream
to Hayden's Creek.

Salmon and shad return
    to crucible of birth; fertilize next generation
born in different waters. In our universe, river
    sentinels, tell us, water is measure of the land,
as blood is for humans' health.

# A Bit Down On Our Luck

I greeted a pair of bluebirds
selecting a nest box in my backyard,
echoing memories of childhood farm
in New Hampshire where
I no longer roam.

Defying starlings, house sparrows,
and wrens, the male
flashed his lapis-colored coat
and contrasting orange finery.

Over time, the female laid five
pale-blue eggs
as the male lilted, trilled,
bobbed, and gestured
clinging to nearby fence.

Until one morning, I heard
the male's fierce cry,
I found his mate in the nest box
limp, with one drop of blood on her head.
Under her warm breast lay
the five pale-blue eggs
cooling fast
as brown thrasher's harsh call
rang out.

# American Woodcock

Near father's pasture of woodland
buttonbush and alder
when sap runs from maple trees,
a male woodcock
mottled like paisley
sweeps over me as I catch
his oversized eyes.

He spins into corkscrew flight
uttering a shrill challenge,
with wings twittering
weaving skyward,
*peeants* intersperse with warbles
floating below.

His bill points downward
as he plummets out of the sky
catches himself and zigzags down:
twitters, whistles, and wheels
into his mate's embrace.

Together they stamp-dance feet
catching earthworms
on damp ground.

Three months later,
bullets sting the air,
his mate flees,
two hatchlings clutching
at her breast between her legs
as other woodcocks fall

grasped by hunters' dogs.
Hurling herself toward the copse,
she plunges into shadows.

Sheltered by canopy of quaking aspen,
a rare spotted turtle crawls on
as the last of twilight burns crimson.

# Sanguinaria Canadensis, Bloodroot

At edge of wildwoods, bloodroot
beneath lingering snow,
devoted to its location,
catching up with itself
on the concert stage
of warbling wood thrushes.

Deeply lobed dark-green
leaves huddle over cream flower
embracing the bud
until rising above it.
Rootstocks' crimson juice
used by Native Americans
for war paint.
Sometimes Indian ladies
discolored gentlemen's linen
with its red liquid.

Once some sprang up
from rootstocks under stone wall
when I, as a child patrolled
for wild flowers and found them
at the peak of their glory,
a clutch
of Venus's wine cups.

I circle wider
make my rounds farther
to locations
that once held creamy beauty
now verging on extinction,
my childhood companions
and sustainers.

# A Day's Climb on the Coast of Cornwall

Back-packing
like the tin, copper and iron-ore miners
of times past, I scramble up cliffs,
over rugged footpaths and wild terrain
of Bodwin Moor and Land's End.

How many miners' wives, children,
horses, donkeys
scarred the terrain crisscrossing
and leaving indelible writings on hillsides,
impressed marks not erased by greenery?

After rain-rinsed day, a blue-orchid sky:
sunbathed, commanding Atlantic,
waves thrusting against headlands
cloudscapes,
hedgerows of moors,
granite tors on hilltops,
citadels of miners' buildings.

Slate, serpentine, and basalt
erode, decline and rise in new patterns
of carnglaze rock piles polished by the ocean.

Toads and frogs haunt salt marsh plants.
Below cliff nesting guillemots, auks and fulmars
Stand by as hatchlings fly out of view.

Years and distances disappear.

## At Ocean's Edge of Peggy's Cove

Sun silvers St. John's steeple.
Some gnarled pines left
where Micmacs wigwamed
and swept soil away
into vast silver-blue ocean.

A purple pitcher plant
bends its head seducing
a green fly like a lobster trap
and periwinkles shut doors
as a least tern clutches a sand eel.
Limpets and barnacles stand up
to pummeling surf.

In years past, when the run
was on for herring and mackerel,
survivors had squatter's rights.
Other creatures struggle today
near ocean's edge.
Salmon hide by shore
clutching smaller ones
with talons of eagle sunk
on salmon's back.

Next year, some fishermen say herring
will return. A cove of shifting views;
white washed the lighthouse stands.
Sandpipers in transit
from nesting grounds move on.

Plovers turn in unison
as host of shorebirds satiate
for South American flight.
I wonder about their mystery....
Each season, I ponder how
some make it, year after year
and worry about the many
who don't return.

# Hummers in the Fast Lane of Costa Rican Rain Forest

On veranda of Savegre River Inn
   tropical warmth embraces,
      an invitation to a treasure trove

of *sun angel* hummingbirds:
   gray-tailed mountain gems,
      magnificents, scintillants,

violet sabrewings, mountain gems,
   green-violet ears,
      fiery-throated, rufous-tailed
         and crowned wood nymphs.

They scan surroundings,
   glean nectar without landing
      steal flies from spider webs;

suck hibiscus blossoms,
   heliconias, coral trees
      and passion flowers.

Spinning back and forth, up and down,
   some bathe in leaves' flowers
      reflecting the sun like rare gems

in jewelry stores.
   Green- violet ears shoot from perches
      like flying arrows

catch sight of females
   disappear in close chases
      showing off dazzling hues.

*One hummer noses into a power dive*
    *hurtles downward, wings a blur*
        *streaks upward above female*

*perches with crown feathers flared*
    *sings loudly as they mate on the wing*
        *then shifts in flight while I blink.*

*She hovers at scarlet passion flower, twirling with*
    *blossoms. They hang motionless*
        *in lose cluster and woo the watchers.*

*Knowing what they mean to us,*
    *I can feel their wings hypnotically humming*
        *this richly dawning day.*

# Prevailing

I found them at the edge of the land

    where still unpaved
    unsmirched.

Crocuses, in necklaces of clover green,

    bowing down
    to touch earth.

Tips of petals touched with emeralds

    ahead of themselves,
    bulbs packed away

for another Spring like some people

    always looking ahead,
    stalwart even in late snow.

# Pacific Coast Rain Forest

Deep into the ancient
forest to primeval,
virgin Sitka spruce and Douglas fir,
I sniff red cedar,
pine-scented, moist air.

Above me
a flying squirrel with wings spread out
like some exotic bat glides down
to truffles on forest floor.

Eye-to-eye a banana slug
brownish-yellow slithers in rich earth.
A colonnade of seedlings
and red-capped
lichens thrive on nurse log.

And farther on in fog and clouds
of Mount Olympus, past clearings
of blue-gray glacial melt water,
a restless bull elk adorned
with rack of antlers
drinks in the creek.

Salmon run, frayed fins battered,
humped bodies twisted against currents.
Their lips clamp shut, never again to eat.
Eagles and raccoons, salmon and elk
affirm the forest's network of life.

Rich, cinnamon-brown
marbled murrelet with beige weskit
under filigreed steel-blue sky
sails off like a flycatcher
whisking over my head.

# Hammonasset Salt Marsh at Winter Solstice

Under a winnowing wind,
in flat lands of stillness
a muskrat in waterproof
coat roams out of mound home.

In winter-day cold with no snow melt
my eyes absorb
the brackish waterways
of reborn nature, gathering in
on a late December day.

Salt marsh spartina turns
from tawny brown to golden green
struggling to emerge.
Shafts of apricot sun break
through eiderdown clouds.

Stalking in the shadows, I sniff out
a great blue heron prehistoric –looking
swathed in slate gray with a glint
of blackish eyes, hunched over in
stalks of sedge and sheaves of reeds.
My eyes to his.
With spear-like beak, what morsel
can he find?

In the high spartina,
a pair of American bitterns spy-hop
blending in with brown stripes nuanced
to stalks of grass,

beaks and eyes upward
among the leafy bayberry
and winter-sheared
rosa rugosa.

# Under Strangler Fig Boughs

Noon sun filters
in remaining patch
of woodland trees
shading coffee plantation.

A strangler fig tree
in deadly hug girdles a palm
hosting food for frugivores.
Our eyes strain
in humid air
to scan a birdathon manna.

An enveloping heart
of strangler fig
festoons sun-tinted
flycatchers, chestnut-sided
warblers, hard-to-see seedeaters,
tanagers and euphonias.
Three turquoise cotingas
perch; pull naturalists
forward with scopes.

Remaining solitary on bough
secretive dove-like birds,
are velvet blue
with patches tinged purple.
Glowing in light, they splay
indigo wing feathers.

In memory, plumage: iridescent
turquoise, cobalt azure,
royal like blue of Sargasso Sea.

Swirling, other birds call
in different directions
as our life lists swell
like frog's chorus
from bromeliads in cloud forest.

# Giant Tortoises on Galapagos

Before pirates, no one harmed them;
    then oil hunters and crews of predators
attacked. Death prevailed leaving
    hollow shells.

Giant tortoises like lava boulders
    bluish-black, dome-shaped and saddle
backed, amble over mossy lagoon
    among forests of prickly-pear cacti.

Male and female stare at me with mouths
    dripping leaves. Antediluvian giants
gather moss and lichens. I stand head high,
    buttressed blinking in understanding.

Now and then, one pulls head into armor.
    Others snap branches, exhale,
hiss, tear cacti, and scratch ground
    with reptile feet.

From nesting grounds of red earth,
    newly hatched babies make it out.
Flipper-like legs stretch frantically,
    for foothold on rocky, volcanic soil.

Coastward, females take journey downhill
    after struggling to lay eggs
and Lonesome George, last off his line
    at 170 remains a bachelor
waiting for a mate.

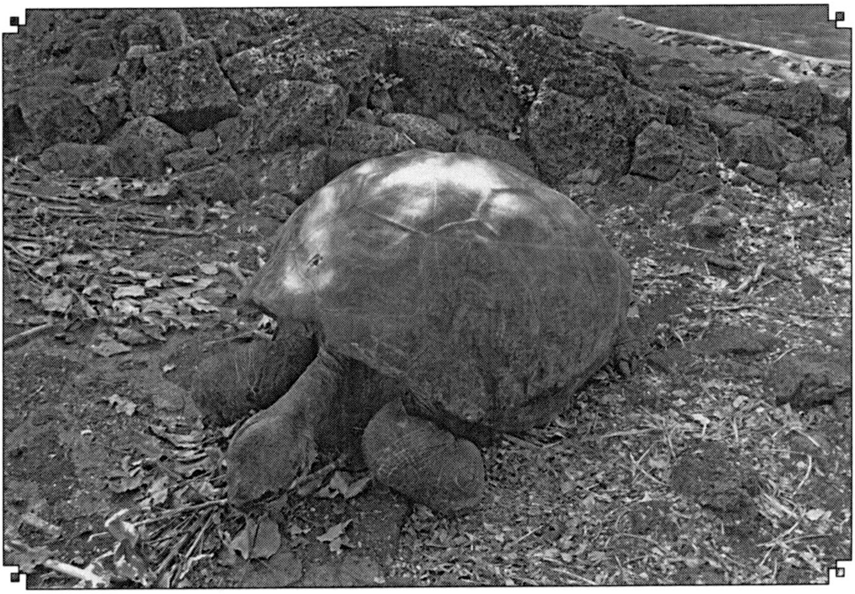

# An Acorn Whistle for Bethany Wanderers

No high-tech razzmatazz here.
No laser beams shining to Elysium fields.
Only Bethany Wanderers with
muted halos stepping along in a tribal order
on the Norfolk Trail.
Following Barrie and Steve whose gifted
fingers like Rumpelstiltskin's make gold
from straw.

Viewing the trees a flying carpet of color,
we rise above the hill to Roosevelt's hunting
lodge, witnessing chestnut and elm,
butternut and hemlock, attacked by monsters
of cankers and blight, yet still quivering
to redeem life.
Where migrating birds embroider
the sky, lakes and trees, you make
an acorn whistle for us
and point your sacred wand touching
"Fairy Rings," then "Witches Hobble"
and "Dwarf's Fungi," showing us
how Lactarius threads the world together.

Then with winged mane, the flight
of Pegasus, in the forest
where genies from a spineless kingdom
rule the earth.

# Florida's Blue

Sitting on a driftwood log watching ripples
by a river of Big Pine Key near an old bridge,
I spot a rare living creature,
a cobalt blue butterfly shimmers swiftly
above blossoms of prickly pear.
She sips nectar from red clover like pinot
noir. Luminous turquoise wings glide, sanctify
and magnify sunlight. She rides a Ferris wheel
of air soaring away making her last stand.
Nearly extinct from pesticides, she clings to fragile
existence in blossoming plants that sprout
on coral sand in shadows of abandoned railroads.

*How did she find her way here?*
Even though mates are gone; she hunts, feeds
and does as she has always done before we
arrived. An echo of voice remains, *Survive,
Survive, Survive*, in small fluttery passings.

# THE JADE BOWER

# Swept Away by Monarchs

Like cliffhangers, they pop out of pupas, bleary-eyed,
tremble on leaves, shiver and bask in sunlight
with orange cloaks, velvet black veins, dotted curbsides,
they pump fluid through wings to undergo flight.

With thousands of eyes monarchs see rainbows;
ultraviolet light guides them where they're bound
en route to Mexican highlands where fir trees grow
on updrafts of air, gliding to warm winter ground.

My mind engraved with most spectacular sight
as I watch thousands sip at oyamel café.
When roosting trees are cut, some clusters freeze at night;
others nectar on milkweed and thistle buffet.

Next spring, if they survive their wintering state,
they wake, bring joy back again, soaring for a mate.

## Gifts of the Season

For this sacred time of winter solstice,
snow whispers, drops softly to earth.
Gifts are tucked away underground,
under snow, under stars.

Presents unwrap themselves before
my eyes-morning, a sunrise softly silver
with clouds of pearl colors.

Sunsets later stretch day time.

Wild birds: scarlet, tawny, carob, rose, olive
flash through trees, swooping close.

Signature of mouse prints in the snow.

On the beach other gifts of waves
push up and sweep, push up and sweep,
against the sand,
and opalescent seashells rise with the tide.

New tides run within me, cycles of sleep
and crystal sharp awareness,
cycles keyed to sun,
to moon, to the universe.

Crystals on every twig, shining in halos
around lamplights.

Frost tangles grapevine and bull briar.
Ice crackles, flexes with frozen frogs
on bottom of pond.

In the woods, under frosted ground,
spore cases reach above velvety green
mosses. Fiddlehead ferns unchanged
since ancient times prepare.

Unwrap the endless presents on the ground,
in trees, and under stars.

## Wangari Muta Maathai

Arrested, jailed, beaten unconscious, still Maathai
refused to eat white snake root, turned her back on
Daniel Moi, *Elder of the Burning Spear who*
would bulldoze the land. Instead she hurled

herself skyward, first to see sun rise and twined
the web of life with immortal hands and golden tongue.
With only a few shillings in her pocket,
she kicked a hole in her cocoon and founded

the Green Belt Movement; freeing peasants to plant
thirty million trees in desiccated land, offering
fruit and clean water for her people. As she climbed
Mount Kenya, her arms, magic wands guided trees

into place. With a hundred thousand kindred spirits,
she stood in front of a bright blue podium at the summit
of a mountain close to heaven. On her braids, the king
arranged the Nobel Peace Prize crown.

Tears in eyes, she kneeled with hands
on Kenya's soil. Peasants, planters
and farmers will whirl and dance
through trees to ends of years.

# Arrivata, Hawksbills

And take the time to come along with me
to Rancho Nuevo on the sandy berm;
we'll witness ancient nomads return
and herald the turtles' *arrivata*.

Marvel at their heads, marble-patterned,
buffeting waves as ocean surface roils.
Headstrong turtles follow mysterious cravings
when moon, tide, wind, weather align.
Watch as they swipe flippers across their faces;
turtle tears washing away time and threat.
Scutes, mottled yellow, amber, brown,
rare flotilla coming home to upper sand.

Hunted for tortoise shell by many nations,
turtle carapaces more highly prized than ivory.
Market traders roughly grab and heave
fully-grown turtles by flippers
and throw into trucks.
Snorting, green eyes are anguished.
Sunlight drops away.

# Darwin's Enchanted Kingdom

(Villanelle)

Darwin, titan of Enchanted Isles
A full moon glows on fish-filled seas.
A force through islands drives evolution's might.

Ponderous tortoises exhale deep sighs.
In no world but Eden could such creatures be.
Darwin, titan of Enchanted Isles

Cactus finches plunge beaks into succulent meals.
Tide pools are play pens for sea lions that tease.
A force through the islands drives species' right.

Cormorants stunted wings lose power of flight.
Over lava, scarlet crabs with stalked eyes
scatter. Darwin, titan of Enchanted Isles

On volcanic rocks he finds golden butterflies
and hundreds of sun-bleached Palo Alto trees.
A force through the islands reveals gleams of light.

His studies in Galapagos explain species' life styles.
Tropic birds pirated by frigates live lives of unease.
Darwin, titan of Enchanted Isles
A force through Galapagos drives evolutions might.

# Stand Alone Cedar at Hammonasset

In the park, that has endured
near my house for over a hundred years,
a weathered eastern red cedar
reaches out across a coiled stream
near a gathering of six others.

Sculpted by wind
and spokes of sunlight;
at ease with wings, humans
and four-legged creatures.
Honeycomb web of roots dip
Into dwellings of frogs, toads,
and salamanders.

Warblers in spring slice air above
gleaning insects but leave
the mourning cloak butterflies
bursting from branches. Needles
fall; scent the fresh soil like spruce
remembrance of childhood campfires.

In fall, I turn to listen to a mockingbird's
song ebb and flow across the marshlands
repeating its melody
singular with tone and color.

I smooth the soft needles, some cleared
by nocturnal creatures, and hum
with song sparrows. They gather
cedar's blueberry-like cones, blooming
like passion buds from bending branches.

THE JADE BOWER

I'll bind with this lone cedar
into hallowed ground
seeking out other red cedar roots.

# Morning Sojourn with Frogs

In woodland pond
quiet sanctuary among alders,
cattails velvet-brown,
lemon-hued sun above water lilies.

Recollection of childhood
bringing home
translucent frog's eggs-
black bellies to heads.

I slid them
from bucket into back yard pond
as they squirmed
among saffron-gold karp
and scarlet koi.

In breadbasket of algae,
green-blue frogs
humped in tunnels pitching warnings
to a muskrat above.

One day tiny limb buds
formed into coiled hind legs.
Tails shrunk and disappeared.
Front legs unfolded over gills; tadpoles
sprouted teeth, jaws and tongue.
Metallic gold eyes protruded from sockets.

Today, morning rings with frog songs;
low-pitched call like distant pounding
on wood and banjo notes,

*t-chung, t-chung, t-chung*
of woodlands;
a united spirit of frogs' nobility.

# Teardowns South of Route One

Landed gentry and lord-of-the-manor
types; some investment bankers, hedge fund
operatives and insurance
CEO's wanted a newer, super-sized
mansion.

(Soon the 1970's colonial would see
its final day.)

The equipment operator wearing dust
mask jerked John Deere excavator,
wreaked destruction;
idling its yellow nemesis, spewed
plumes of smoke into blew sky
propelling its holy mission.

Volkswagen size bucket and T-Rex
limbs tore shingles into splinters
as metal gutters shrieked.

Siding and debris filled basement.
Shutters and awnings fluttered
over foundation.
Steel tentacles clawed apart children's
bedrooms leaving wall to wall carpets
flapping.
Bucket dropped fireplace bricks filling
green/black coffins.

The claw rose and toilets exploded
into internment, struck copse of maples,
oaks, and dogwoods and buried
log pile. Dust motes from gargantuan
hole backlit by sunlight left big memory
chasms.

The center gaped wide
like a smoking caldera.

# Crows and Sycamores

**(painting by James Cook)**

Untouched by humans,
deep in the woods,

full sunlight bathes white-pearl
and golden sycamore.

Burgundy, amber-yellow leaves
massage ground;

set off by shades
of lichened rocks

and blades of shrubs
on the ridge.
Musty odor of composting leaves

Caw, caw, cawing of crows,
midnight-black forms in breeding
livery spotlight silver-gray
of smoked-glass sky.

On trunks and branches of sycamores,
patches of pearl-gold change shape
and colors with every angle.

Breezes blow through, rustle,
rearrange crows and leaves.

# Sinking Boot Steps

Stacks of data collections of waste and storm water
reviews shuttle from town to state. In EPA offices
papers just shuffle from hands around departments.
Storms of arguments yet building continues.
Sediment of road sand flows into salt marshes
suffocating oyster and clam beds.

Alpine glaciers melt, crash, send sea
level along coast over tarmac. Fractured rocks
from wave-battered sea rumble. Trees with
branches stretch like mammoth arms
on shrubs of tidal wetlands. A trailer cab rests
on uplifted house catching a speed boat
flung up by waves. Homes along main arteries
slide into the Gulf. Condos collapse on flood plains
as waste water washes on lawns and climbs stairs.
How violent the night is!
Mayors, Selectmen and Town Planning and Zoning
shaken awake never imagined they would have
to be the first evacuated and never suspected
it would happen like this.

# Lake District's Dry Stone Walls

Under a heather sky as morning breaks,
we trek the dales and clamber up the fells
near tarns and keeps and old stone walls.
Our boots crunch bracken, ferns and moss,

while sheep with sidelong looks make way to let
us pass. Here stone age farmers, Celts and Norse
summoned spirits to layer slate stones, crossing fields
with Herdwick sheep, on high moors. Listen!

I hear the Knights whisper. Like the sorcerers
of Hadrian's Wall, Stonehenge and the pyramids,
they quarried rocks for dry-stone walls, clutching
stones of quartz and granite. As before, I hear

the Knights whisper. They tell us tales of those
who built stone walls high in the fells in wind,
and rain and sun; who sculpted slate on stone
mid fragrant fern, praying to some ancient force
that was and is and shall be evermore.

THE JADE BOWER

# Riding the Chariot to the Divine: Legendary Lord God Bird Sighted

In bottomland forest of cypress and tupelo
slate-colored swamps spread tributaries.
Spotted muck thickened with moss
held cottonmouth snakes, lizards, alligators.
Deltas meandered into slopes and silent sinkholes.
Ivory-bills drummed, tapped, pried, peeled bark,
whammed away, slurped beetle larvae and sent
chips flying. They banded together in mud-stained
oaks, stunted sycamore, and palmetto hung
with muscadines, over fern screens
and Spanish moss. Nests of wood storks,
barred owls, ibis, and egrets cradled in branches.
Here the woodpeckers watched stars blink out above.

Regarded as sacred, protector of children;
gods with mighty powers who brought rain.
Ivory bills lifted wings, reigned over forest
estates until brought down by natives in war dresses
of crests, necklace of bills pointed outwards.
Bills and bodies buried with Indian warriors
and princes. Colonial merchants used feathers
for currency; sold dry skins for museum specimens.
Frontiersmen shot and stuffed them
for Victorian parlors.

Trophy hunters dangled ivory bills for sale,
used bodies for money pouches, shot them
from nests; crushed birds' heads
for some elusive power.

In forest of Louisiana, overnight,
working ahead of legislation,
Singer and Chicago Lumber Companies
bulldozed grand monarchs
hollowed out swampy lands.

Trees screamed down
tearing off limbs
spanning millions of acres.
Only a lone female was last seen
in Singer tract before they vanished.

And then, decades later
on a Mississippi bayou,
a rare-bird lover kayaking hears raps,
and tooting calls,
high notes of clarinet
and *peent, peent, peent* chorus.

It flies across his path
lifts three-foot wings
swings upward to dead tupelo.

Graced in glossy blue- black; gleams
of fluorescent white trailing wings,
amber eyes, long-neck, scarlet crest blazing,
ivory dagger shoots across like a flaming arrow.
The kayaker weeps and shouts in awe,
*Lord God, look at that bird!*

For thirty years, it may have secretively lived
in bottomland forest, played to a mate,
raised its flaming crest in circling flights.

We need rare birds
to have a new heaven on earth when a man
weeps at a flash of white wing, ivory dagger
and flaming cockade.

# Libretto for Spirit Bear Wilderness of British Columbia

In heartland of Great Bear rainforest
spirit bears find refuge in cathedral trees;
other grizzlies, black, and cream- coloreds
tramp forest trails scrabbling on ground
grasping lichens and berries.

Not likely to yield the trail,
we lay eyes on two cream-coloreds.
They wind us, smell our scent;
send out hair-raising calls.

*A raven deity whitened*
*spirit bears, so all of land would remain pristine.*

Silver-scarlet salmon jump streams in lagoon.
Spirit bear wades in, without a ripple
clutches Chinook, throws out to newly- born cubs.

*Salmon live under the earth;*
*are reborn as salmon-people.*

Silver- blue, bright orange and yellow
circling faces with bark-colored eyes,
a ghost bear from another world
rears up on hind legs.

*We must court the bear's goodwill.*

In retreat, pods of porpoises
and sea lions toss, splash stones

and pebbles across glacial rivers.
Sounds of natives blend arctic
breezes and shifting sands.

In Koeye river valley, dressed
in button blankets,
mothers, fathers, children, grandparents
chain to logging machines.

Do you watch in horror as clear cutters
and miners remove mountain tops,
plunder graves
bury rivers that embody spirit bear
and salmon spirits?
Godess trees wash up like white bones.
Some trophy species lost, lie unburied.

*We cannot sever the cord of life
from the land. Bones of our ancestors are
grounded in soil.*

# Goldfinch Days

"After Milosz"

She sang of summer months in youth
    raking, loading and storing hay.

She rejoiced: in goldfinch-colored days
    roaming woods for mayflowers and lady slippers

In eloquence of her Protestant preacher
    and candlelight services

In evenings, dancing the twist and fox trot
    at Community Grange Hall

In rainbow trout at Highland Lake
    and swimming by forested islands

In visiting Hammonasset tidal salt marshes
    watching shore and sea birds

In discovering channeled whelks and horseshoe
    crabs shelled in mystery

In finding mermaid's purses, sea urchins, sand
    dollars and fiddler crabs on Atlantic beaches

In high tide when the moon is full
    sleeping on a bed of hay

In orchards, fields and whitewashed
    milking barn for cows

In feasting on strawberries, peaches, cherries
    and wild blueberries

In books that opened tunnels
    and scents of apple blossoms.

## Orcas' Opera

(Resurrection Bay, Prince William Sound)

We find them now in embracing pods:
females, males, juveniles,
calves, aunts, uncles, cousins, orphans
and *grammies* in matrilineal group.

A whole super pod assembly share
prey of Chinook, halibut and porpoise
hunting seals and cavorting in waves
larger than themselves.

High-pitched squeaks,
squeals, whistles, syncopated clicks,
chirps, tail slaps, a concert of calling
and singing orcas.

Tangy scent of saltwater
lingers with whiff of fish as porpoises arc
higher and higher in leaps around hull.

Rain and ocean spray mingle
with captain's voice as horned puffins,
red-legged kittiwakes, long-tailed jaegers
race from sharp-walled fjords
and hanging glaciers.

Juveniles poke heads above sea and scan
surroundings: waving and slapping tails
and flippers,
lobtailing, breaching, spy hopping,
chasing and rubbing against one another,

the males extruding
grey-pink penises.
Others rest lining up side-by-side.
Some dive and surface a mile away.

Icebergs drip in mistiness from rocky
pinnacles. Fountains of bubbles
rise as blowholes
and dorsal fins line up
above choppy waves.

At home,
orca whales dive into my dreams
of opera shows
in Resurrection Bay.

# Golden Frogs

Atlantic lowlands on one side
Pacific Ocean on the other.

In *elfin* cloud forest of twisted trees,
gnarled, broken and draped in mosses
haven of rarest creatures,
only one place on earth.
in little patch
of high rain forest.

Males dress in intense golden-orange;
females, brown, mottled green, black and red
like red-eyed tree frogs.

After the first Easter rains, males entice,
swarm around, mob, hug females in puddles.

Each male wrestles to be first rolls
into full golden ball with females.

In water filled pools of bromeliads
little soup balls with tadpoles huddle inside
within the cradle of a cluster of jelly.

When born, mothers carry tiny toads
piggy-back style
to shelter of bromeliad home
high in canopy
giving a warning
of what could devour them.

Farmers want to use frog's home for pasture
dooming golden toads into the abyss
from where no creature ever returns.

# Jesus Christ Lizard of Esquinas

Beside the shore of a natural pond,
shimmering with sunshine, a caimon
lies-in wait.

Jesus Christ lizard, tree-dwelling
basilisk prances light-footed,
scampers across the water

raising arms and legs for balance,
splaying toes on hind legs. He barely
escapes from mottled brown

cat-eyed snake in disguise
slithering down lianas.

Pouncing out of the lake, flinging water aside
the lizard repels mouth of grasping caimon.

Every creature needs one another
in lowland rain forest of Costa Rica.

And I wonder if humankind realizes

there is a cry from the heart
over the rainforest creatures' homes of loss.

# Anatomy of Alaska Landscape

Beyond rumbling of the thunderstorm
amidst fragments of glaciers over moraine,
earthwork's sloping side cascades from cliffs.
A beam of sunlight breaks through, turning
falls to glimmer of silver through rivers of Psalms.
A raven on totem pole flutters sun-struck wings
above forests of moss squishing under my boots.
Ferns, mosses, fungi, beetles, and salamanders
gather and nourish in rotting wood of fallen hemlocks.

Beyond icebergs changing to silver-gray,
mountain glaciers glow and melt. Thunderous
waves shush off cliffs. Beyond silvery- black basaltic
pillars, marbled murrelets lay eggs in moss of Sitka spruce.
I discover a homeland where no bones are wasted
and the forest hums.

# Iceland Summer

Amid June warmth, harbor, harp and hooded
seals slither home. Blue-gray and crisp-
black dolphins take spins,
sunbathing, acrobating, airlifting
and splashing from sea depths.

Splay-footed puffins
strut, beating wings on rock cliffs
as reincarnated monks clasping feet in prayer.
In courting dress, puffins entice mates
by come-hither gestures; pair off
on lava-layered cliffs.

Harlequin ducks and pink-footed geese
enter their element, forge bonds
with ceaseless fluttering.
Chicks chirp from inside eggs;
hatch
and take daring leaps over edge of cliffs.

Arctic terns with elegant wing spans
and designer tails glide and soar,
light and buoyant.

And you can listen
from the shore and envision
rare species returning home.

CAROL LEAVITT ALTIERI

# I've Been Traveling on that Interstate Highway

With fellow commuters
following the Siren Song of the city,
I wear charms and amulets around my neck
and secure a horseshoe on my seat.

We are drawn together
facing quadruple headlights
as incandescent light spills down
on the early morning throughway
in adagio rhythm, like camel trekking
in Australia's Outback.

Monstrous trucks, road trains
gasoline drums, orange- highway trucks,
bulldozers, car trailers, trailer trucks,
18 wheelers,
shift like giant boulders
on deserts of sand.

Off by the side of I-95,
a wisteria vine holds a spruce tree
hostage and plastic bags
clutch the Staghorn Sumac.

Demons of road warriors
weave in and out of triple lines;
like road suckers, they overtake,
wipe out, bear down and hold others
hostage. Manacled. Shanghaied!

Cars roll into ditches;
trains jackknife as police
in multi- colored cars flash strobe lights.
Lanterns lure vessels onto coastal rocks.

With my little foot, I extend my body
pull back, undulate, and expand a half-mile,
retract and uncoil around obstacles.

## Commander and Spotted Owls

He used to be high up in the navy,
now retired, but still duty-driven.
At dawn, he climbs up rocky terrain,
to make camp by the Douglas firs.

We clamber after him up Cave Creek
Canyon as he disappears into shadows
with backpack of frozen road kill
leaving us fumbling for footholds.

He tenders spotted owls to protect
them. We have been *pishing*
to hear their voices,
but he shushes us, not to disturb
owlets slumber.

Then we hear *hoo-hoo-hoooooing!*

We catch sight of two owls roosting
on branches, the male with his wings
warming his mate. Their bodies packed
like woven jugs, in rich chestnut,
tawny, streaked and mottled.
The commander must trek up to hide their
own places, having invested
his whole retirement
in forming a triad with them.

And we know this now,
he will save spotted owls from falling

over the cliff
in woodland home.
We will honor him always,
for here, in Cave Creek Canyon
the owls are reborn
from oblivion.

## Shoreline Showdown

Stretching to the river, it's
the great abbey, Hammonasset,
landscape of green-gold marshland
and woodlands visited with warblers
that set you off
in a rainbow trance.

Selectmen, computing taxes, selling out
elderly citizens and x-y-z ers
bound to shell-shaped land
and a community full
of newly-awakened passion.

Real estate developers
show off utopian renderings,
always getting what they want—
tearing the land's flesh
and siphoning life blood,
turning their backs
on living community.

While they bring scams,
we join legions of soul-crushed,
threatened creatures.

Outsiders, rich with starched shirts
and bottomless pockets
even now plotting
to bulldoze and backhoe.

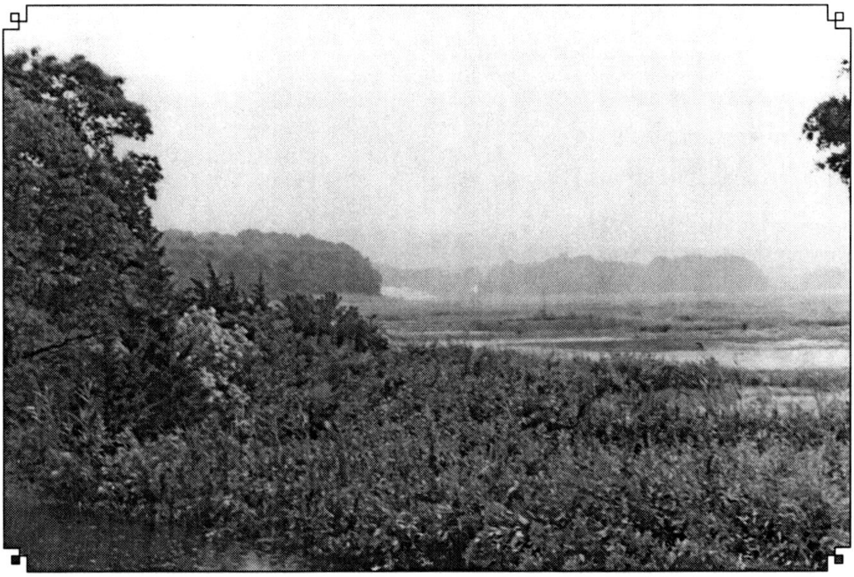

# View from Our Backyard

I thought it was a demilitarized zone
as between North and South Korea,
a haven for woodland birds: hermit thrushes,
rose-breasted grosbeaks
and black-throated blue warblers.

For all my life,
I thought it would remain,
lush woodland that sheltered
the emerald jewels of summer;
earth hues in autumn,
a playground for chipmunks, squirrels
and foxes.

Until one day....
I thought frost came dropping like death
browning everything in sight
nine whole acres—bare,
nothing left
except strangled tree roots.

All night, the bulldozer and crane
must have done their work in the darkness,
now reclining
with guards trumpeting warnings to trespassers.

The shagbark hickory where I gathered nuts
remains in my thoughts,
and the creek runs red with mud.

The homeless family of foxes in the darkness
prowled the neighborhood
breathing their last
before being struck on Route 1.

Dispossessed animals like phantoms
clandestine in shadows of condos.

# How Far Does the Poison Sink?

Bhopal

Each year, since 1984
    survivors burn an effigy
of Union Carbide's CEO from a fork lift
    as they march through Bhopal
demonstrating against the explosion that unleashed

poison clouds of methyl isocyanate
    to wells and reservoirs.
No groundwater found to quench thirst
    sky black with soot; scumbles
of chemical ash like hoar frost
    buried the ground.
Every tree branch screamed down.

Cacophony of cries,
    ears deafened
Nostrils raw with burning,
    tongues sour with mercury,
thousands fled from stinging pesticides.
    Human legs sucked into toxic sink holes.
Hundreds trampled to death
    those left, stared from empty sockets.

Far away in the Hamptons CEO
    plays golf, attends dinner parties, defends space
downgrades homicide charges
    ignores arrest warrants. He is quietly serene;
folds hands in evening prayer.

Acid rain falls on the earth
    where only stomas of white Amanitas grow.

# Mountain Top Removal

(Dedicated to victims of Utah mine disaster, August 2007)

In shade of Appalachian forest
    an ovenbird sang vespers.
Under French blue haze
    sunlight glints struck the understory
of rich bottomland loam.

As a child, I seduced songbirds
    watched cerulean warblers
with velvet blue crowns nest in cavities.
    Aspen, birch trees lined rivers, rustling
leaves, billowing crowns,
    brown-eyed Susans caressed my legs.
Here I honeycombed;
    countless butterflies flittered.

Before mine owners bombed, bulldozed,
    beheaded entire mountain tops
murdering forests, stones, streams,
    stripping off angiosperms, gymnosperms
flaying moss from layers of shale-sandstone-
    tearing out coal
from osteoporotic bones of cracked earth,
    leaving plant less valleys
cracked house foundations
    sweeping away cemeteries, lifting caskets.
Topsoil, sediment buried
    hundreds of miles of rivers below

tattooed with dynamite's orange poison.
   A black soot hovers over earth's craters.
How does a lover rise above
   such catastrophe?

# In Brazil's Rainforest Tribal Chief Marimo Fights Loggers

*We were born in the middle of the forest
and know every corner of it.*

>  Wrapped in tropical warmth,
>  toucans and capybaras
>  play out rainforest hymns
>  where palm and mahogany
>  seedlings seek the sun.

>  Resurrection ferns grow on
>  massive trees and ancient
>  trunks.
>  Scarlet, lobster claw
>  heliconia creates a cradle
>  for its creatures.

>  The strangler fig vine festoons
>  around its cecropia tree in
>  deadly embrace.

>  Water droplets gleam on leaves
>  of tropical orchids.

*We rely on the spirits of the forest to protect us.*

>  Violet-crowned wood nymphs
>  sip nectar from passion flowers
>  and call to females from song
>  perches.

Screams of howler, capuchin
monkeys, and red macaws
resound from bamboo, papaya,
banana plants and palm.

Fields
of shade-grown coffee
are revived.

Clear- cutter loggers with AK-
47's put orange fuse- like
flagella through rivers
after shaving away top soil.

With bow and arrow Marima
seizes logging truck,
forces invader to flee; throws
chains over logging roads.

We'll continue on our trail
of resplendent quetzals.

Resurrection fern grows on
ancient trunks as Morpho
butterfly soars and flashes
fluorescent blue.

A royal flycatcher raises his
spectacular crest of orange and
green unfolding leafy parasols to
the sky.

# Catch the Day's Celestial Farewell at Hammonasset

As the sea thrusts upward,
we saunter
over boardwalk
and catch the aurora borealis
of braided streams:
emerald, quartz, gold
and ruby, vivid
as folk dances
renewed by waves on
Long Island Sound.

Horizons subtle and brilliant blend
and shift skyward.
Earthshine colors merge, pierce
the sky, tint meadow
and marsh.

Above, roseate terns and piping plovers
navigate by Polaris
as eider ducks with golden eyes
raise wings in farewell
and late song sparrows
hop through
marshland *rosa rugosa*.

Sound waters swoosh, drift
upstairs and down.

Striped bass and blues arrive
in groups like visitors

and depart soon after. Three
rivers here
merge with the sea,
nurture layers
of crabs, clams, and mussels.

We wander along
like sanderlings, in shifting patterns
navigating struggles,
stretching our vision, shining
with reflected light
framed by sunset and spinning earth.

## Some Resonating Notes

Consider the once pristine refuge
in Patagonia where shy huemul deer
standing two feet tall
hiding in undergrowth
feed on fallen orchids.

Revere the light brown and dark
cinnamon, velvet guanacos with bright
eyes twisting their necks together.

Admire the jeweled hummingbirds
poised on twisted branches in flurries
of snow.

Tilt your face to view
the long-lived *alerce* trees, conical
giants with red-brown paisley trunks.

Cross the creek over stones and hear
the startling whistle of the Austral pygmy owl.

Now think about these majestic creatures
overcoming hunger pains and loss of shelter
trying to prevail; evolving artifices,

seeking survival from an alien invasion
as they continue to live on the run.

Answer the questions of the natives to know
why their majestic trees are logged away
and the land booby-trapped with craters.

"How does a lover rise above / such catastrophe?" asks Carol Altieri in a poem describing Utah mine owners who "bombed, bulldozed / beheaded entire mountain tops. Whether she is transporting the reader to her childhood home, where "hay stubble haggards / dry for winter, " or crying out in rage against "the slash and burn ones" who seek to destroy the earth she cherishes, Altieri's rich images and vivid metaphors insist that we pay attention, reminding us over and over of the interconnectedness of all living things. As the powerful evidence accumulates, the reader clearly sees the connection between loggers who would destroy Brazil's rainforests, where "violet crowned wood nymphs sip nectar / from passion flowers," and a Connecticut selectman who insists that "birds / must accommodate to our lifestyle," when arguing for the building of condos on a pristine shoreline. Indeed, it is hard to imagine a reader who would not be inspired and moved by Altieri's passionate voice and her deep identification with our planet, hard to imagine someone who would not acknowledge that we too are "the bloodroot bleeding where the oaks fall," and we forget at our peril that "the world works better / when it doesn't lose its pieces." Edwina Trentham

# *Acknowledgements:*

Grateful acknowledgement is made to the editors of the following journals in which poems have appeared, some in slightly rewritten versions:

Whisper in the Woods: Michigan's Nature Journal, Winter 2004, Anthology of New England Writers, 1998, Connecticut Journal, 1995, Connecticut River Review, 1995, Connecticut Review, 1998, Eclectic Rainbows, Family Earth, Southern Connecticut Folio, Monadnock, Moose Bound Press, Massachusetts Journal of Graduate Liberal Studies, Oregon Poetry Journal, Poetry Forum, The Connecticut Writer, The Lowell Pearl, Tributaries, Verse Weavers, Oregon State Poetry Anthology of Prize Winning Poems, 2003, A Journal of Nature Writing, Caduceus, 2004, 2005, Poeticas, 2004, Writers Unlimited , Golden Words, 2005–2006, California Poetry Journal, 2005, Long River Run II, 2006, Connecticut River Review, 2007.

## Special Thanks

I am indebted to Dr. Sue Holloway whom I have been linked in friendship by celebrating the communal intricacies of natures' web of lives. Poet, teacher, historian, critic, journalist and organizer of our writing group, she lived in Stony Creek and Guilford before she passed away in April, 1997.

I would like to thank all my fellow writers for helping me bring the poems into their final forms. Sincere gratitude to all who gave encouragement and stimulated me in many ways and who have been unfailingly helpful: Claire Zogbh, Sally Belenardo, Jane Kellogg, Elizabeth Possidente, Jean Vulte and Gail Kolin.

My abiding thanks to Connie Del Visco, a great artist and deep-rooted friend whom I have known for 46 years. She has planted many trees, flowers and innumerable artistic works.

I am aware of my debt to my first poetry teacher, Tony Connor from Wesleyan University for his artistic gifts of thoroughness, concreteness and originality which have been planted in my poetry.

Special thanks to Dr. Vivian Shipley for continual encouragement and critiques which stimulated my poetry to grow with passion, complexity and imaginative leaps.

My deepest thanks to Edwina Trentham for being a poet of wonders, a true original, for stimulating valuable suggestions and strong creative support as the poetry book took shape, many real sparks of illumination.

Many grateful thanks to Freya Fisher for her excellent photograph of the Isinglass River, Stacy Niedzwiecky for the enchanting Northern Leopard Frog and Audrey Fitting for generous assistance with photography and technology.

Much appreciation to Frank Scott, who very patiently and generously assisted me with technical support services exorcising all evil spirits of Sisyphus. His continual guidance, when I felt enslaved, nipped my destructive tendencies.

In addition, Frank, adult children and grandchildren who affirmed and inspired me to greater insights with accomplishments, interests and disciplined work, who have supported me emotionally all the years and kept me going when I labored in doubt.

# Bio

Carol was awarded the Degree of Advanced Study at Wesleyan University, after receiving a Master's Degree in English and American literature and a Sixth Year Degree in Educational Leadership at Southern Connecticut State University. While there, she received "Graduate Poet of the Year."

In 2005–2006, she received Silver Laureate Award for Poetry by National Senior Poets' Laureate. In 2006, she received First Prize in California State Poetry Contest and in 2007, First Prize in Al Savard Memorial Poetry Contest of the Connecticut Poetry Society and First and Third Prize in Pennsylvania Poetry Contest in 2008.

As recipient of an English Speakers Union's Scholarship, Carol has studied English literature and culture at the University of London for two summers and participated in Yale/New Haven Teachers Institute for six years.

A member of Branford Poets and the Guilford Poets Guild, she is now a retired English and science teacher working as a literacy volunteer. She has published two previous books of poetry, In Beijing, There Are No Dawn Redwoods, The Isinglass River and the third, The Jade Bower, is a present goal.

Aside from spending a great deal of time working for conservation protecting irreplaceable natural resources of Hammonasset Park, River and Biological Reserve, she writes essays, memoirs, letters and poetry. In addition, she enjoys her grandchildren, hiking, birding, traveling, and reading: natural history, essays, poetry, and creative non-fiction.